Making Sense of

THE PLACE NAMES
OF THE
LAKE DISTRICT

by
David Watson

First published in 2009 by
Photoprint Scotland

© David & Rosemary Watson

All rights reserved

ISBN 978-0-9559438-4-3

Photographs by David & Rosemary Watson
Aerial photograph by Simon Ledingham
Graphics and design by Rosemary Watson

Printed and bound by MLG, Glasgow

CONTENTS

INTRODUCTION

What this book is about

To many people, place names are merely a collection of letters and syllables. However, in most languages, names are usually very old and the vast majority of them are descriptive. They often say something about the nature of the landscape. Moreover, when the people who gave the names lived very close to nature, they named almost every nook and cranny, every stream, every rock face, every little summit. Many names relate to the plants, animals and birds which were common in the past.

Other names relate to people who used or owned the land at some time, and some are about how it was used, and frequently how it was changed. The purpose of this book is to open your eyes as you visit the Lake District, and to help you begin to realise that names have meanings, and often reveal things which will enrich your visit.

A mixture of names from different languages

Southern Lake District road signs

Where did the names come from?

Place names are a reflection of the waves of settlers who have arrived in Cumbria over the last 2000 to 3000 years. Some, such as the Vikings, had a profound influence in many areas, whereas others, like the Romans, who, in spite of building Hadrian's Wall, made very little long-lasting impact on the place names of the area. Different settlers spoke different languages, and often they were interested in different sorts of land, settling different areas. They also came from a variety of directions. We shall start by briefly looking at these different contributions.

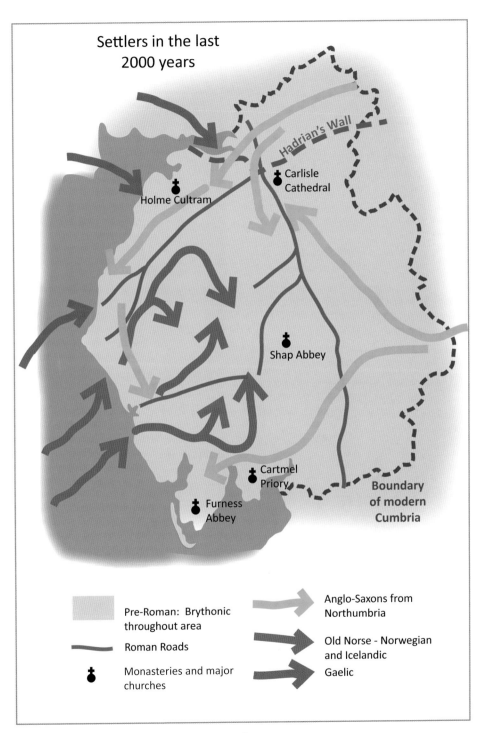

Settlers in the last 2000 years

Hadrian's Wall

Holme Cultram

Carlisle Cathedral

Shap Abbey

Cartmel Priory

Furness Abbey

Boundary of modern Cumbria

Pre-Roman: Brythonic throughout area

Roman Roads

Monasteries and major churches

Anglo-Saxons from Northumbria

Old Norse - Norwegian and Icelandic

Gaelic

Old European

"Old European" is the blanket term used for the ancient languages spoken by the most ancient European inhabitants. These were the folk who gradually moved into northern Europe as the last ice age receded, about 10,000 to 12,000 years ago.

We know almost nothing of the languages of these so-called Palaeolithic folk, nor of their stone age successors, the Neolithic stone circle builders, nor of the Bronze Age folk who followed them.

Many scholars believe that there were three different linguistic strands at this time, one centred in southern Europe, another in northern Europe and another which produced the Celtic languages of the western fringes. Perhaps the most primitive and early names are those of rivers, and it is believed that the elements of some river names may be especially ancient.

Eskdale Beck

Brythonic Celtic

By the time the Romans arrived in the area in the 1st century AD, the inhabitants of western Britain spoke variations of the same language all the way from southern Scotland, through Cumbria, Wales, Cornwall and across the Channel to Brittany. We now call this Brythonic Celtic.

In Cumbria a version we call "Cumbric" was spoken generally until about 500 AD, after which it was gradually ousted by incoming groups. Remnants of Cumbric have stubbornly remained almost until the present, especially in isolated dales.

Some examples include:

> "blen" as in Blencathra
> "pen" as in Penrith
> "crag" as in Friar's Crag
> "esk" as in Eskdale

Penrith Town Centre

The Romans

As in Scotland, the Roman occupation made hardly any impact on the place names of the Lake District. This was largely due to the fact that there were almost no non-military Roman settlements.

The few examples that there are include:

"galava" as in Galava Gate, Ambleside

Property sign using the old Roman name

But they left behind a collection of names.

Examples include:

"mere" as in Buttermere
"ton" as in Broughton and Lorton
"ham" as in Hensingham
"wick" as in Keswick

Moot Hall. Keswick, at night

Old English

From about 600 AD there came an expansion of languages originating on the North European Plain, as new settlers spilled out from the Anglo-Saxon stronghold in Northumbria. They came via the Tyne gap and up the Eden valley, and over Stainmore, following the present route of the A66. Anglo-Saxons occupied much of lowland Britain, but in the Lake District their influence was mainly in the plains around the fringes.

These lowland folk were happiest near the coast and in the valleys, and they made little penetration into the mountains and the dales of Lakeland.

Old Norse

Without a doubt the settlers from Scandinavia, the ones we know as the "Vikings", made the biggest impact on Lake District place names. Popular history identifies them as raiders, rapists and pillagers, but most were farmers, settlers and clearers of the land.

They mainly came originally from Norway, but frequently via Iceland, western Scotland, Ireland and the Isle of Man. They probably arrived first in southwest Cumbria, then penetrating the valleys which were so like their homeland, and eventually the whole of Lakeland. Whichever route they took to get here, we refer to their language as Old Norse.

There are more Old Norse-derived names in the Lake District than from any other language. Some occur scores, even hundreds of times. Clearly the Vikings were the first people to settle the whole of the Lake District. They first came in large numbers in the 9th century, and their influence lasted until the 12th century.

Examples of their influence on names include:

> "..ay" as in Rathay
> "beck" as in Hope Beck
> "dale" as in Borrowdale"
> "force" as in Aira Force
> "gill" as in Sour Milk Gill
> "pike" as in Scafell Pike
> "tarn" as in Sprinkling Tarn
> "thwaite" as in Braithwaite

The signpost for Borrowdale

Gaelic (Goidelic Celtic)

The other form of Celtic is called "Goidelic" or Gaelic, and it is believed the language came originally from Ireland about 1500 years ago, initially probably via Ayrshire and Galloway. Gaelic speakers arrived in Cumbria from the Isle of Man, from Ireland and from Scotland. There are many examples of Gaelic words which are combined with Norse or English, and a few which are pure Gaelic.

Much of this influence is thought to have come via Irish missionaries, though there is also a strong belief that the Norse settlers, having come to Cumbria via Gaelic-speaking areas, often most likely brought a combination of Old Norse-Gaelic names with them.

Typical is "glen" as in Glencoyne.

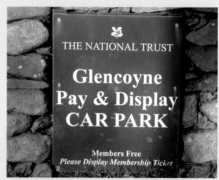

National Trust car park sign at Glencoyne

French and Middle English

Although the language and the place names of the Lake District have gradually been affected by the same Anglicisation process which occurred in the rest of Britain, the actual influence in Cumbria of the Norman invasion was fairly slight, with Norse and Brythonic names generally persisting. This is partly due to the fact that Cumbria did not finally become a permanent fixture to the rest of England until about the end of the 13th century.

The main influence of the French came through the establishment of the great monasteries and abbeys, and the feudal baronies with the takeover of vast tracts of land.

From the 11th century onwards, the old

language was gradually replaced, but the majority of the place names remained, especially deep in the mountains.

Were place names written or just spoken?

As with many local cultures around the world, until the last century or so, many names have only been spoken rather than recorded in writing. When names were written, they often occurred in different spellings, even in the same document. However, many names derived from a thousand years ago are only first seen in writing in the first edition of the Ordnance Survey maps in the 19th century. Before then, they were passed on by word of mouth, down the generations.

In addition, since they were first applied, many names have mutated. Often, names with different origins and meanings, have even converged into similar spellings.

Some names illustrate not only mutation, but also the total ignorance, as now, of the former meaning or indeed meanings of names. One nice example, just outside the national park, is Torpenhow. Each syllable , **...tor, ...pen** and **...how,** has the same meaning, "hill". So in their ignorance, different language groups have ended up with a name meaning "Hill, hill, hill. Where possible it is important to find the earliest written record, and a great debt is owed to the many scholars, most recently Diana Whaley in "A Dictionary of Lake District Place names", who have researched the first known occurrences of Cumbrian names.

The Meaning of Place names

It is not intended here to produce either a detailed or definitive explanation of place names, or to enter into discussion or debate about the origin of names. So there is little discussion in this little book of original sources or of the frequent variation in possible meanings. What this book does is to offer the most likely meaning or meanings for a selection of names, and to suggest the most likely linguistic origins.

Hopefully, readers will wish to take their initial interest further, in which case refer to the short bibliography on page 56, which will allow you to get to grips with more detailed explanations and discussion of Lake District place names.

Generally there is an attempt to explain the main elements of each name and how the meaning of the name has been built up.

How the book is organised

For each letter of the alphabet there is a section divided into three parts:
Lakes and Rivers
Mountains, Fells and Valleys
Towns, Villages,Farms and Areas.

In the explanation of place names, the following code is employed:

B	British/Brythonic
C	Cumbric (the local version of Brythonic)
OE	Old English (Anglo-Saxon)
ON	Old Norse
OFr	Old French
ME	Middle English

COMMON NAMES AND PHRASES

...ay	ON "a"	Pertaining to a river or water. As in *Brathay*.
bank	ME "banke"	A slope. As in *Dowbank*.
beck	ON "bekkr"	The common Cumbrian word for a stream, eg *Coledale Beck*.
barrow	OE "berg"	A rounded, low hill as in *Fellbarrow*.
birk	ON "birki"	Birch tree.
bracken	ME "braken"	Pertaining to the species of fern *Pteridium aquilinum*
brock	OE "brock"	A badger, as in *Brockhole*.
brow	Mod E "brow"	A slope. As in "*eyebrow*"
burn	OE "burna"	A stream, more normally used in Scotland
close	ME "close"	An enclosure or farm
common	OFr "commune"	Unenclosed common land. As with *Grasmere Common*.
crag	G "creag"	The common term used for a rocky outcrop or cliff, eg *High Scarth Crag*.
croft	OE "croft"	A small enclosure
crook	ON "krokr"	Bend in a river
dale	ON "dalr"	Common name for valley, as in *Wasdale*
dodd	ME "dodd"	Rounded hill, as in *Hartson Dodd*.
fell	ON "fjall"	Perhaps the iconic Lakeland name. Used for hills and mountains, as in *Blaewith Fells*.
fold	OE "fald"	Describes a small compound or enclosure, as at *Knipe Fold*.

force	ON "fors"	A waterfall, as in *Aira Force*.
garth	ON "garor"	An enclosure or farm, as in *Grasgarth*.
gill	ON "gil"	Refers to a ravine or gorge with a stream. As in *Longhouse Gill* and many others.
glen	Br/G "glinn/ glean"	Describes a mountain valley. Most common in Scotland, with a few in the Lake District, as at *Glencoyne* and *Glenridding*.
grise...	ON "grise"	Relating to a place associated with pigs. As in *Grisedale Pike*.
ground	OE "grund"	Describes someone's farm, as in *Roger Ground*.
hall	OE "hall"	Originally referred to the manor house. Today more likely just a farm, as in *Crook Hall*.
how(e)	ON "haugr"	Mountain or hill, as in *Great How*.
holm(e)	ON "holmr"	Island or land more or less surrounded by water, as in *Silver Holme* in Windermere.
ling/lyng	ON "lyng"	Heather-covered, as at *Ling Fell*.
low	ME "low"	Usually meaning "low" or "lower" as opposed to "high" or "higher".
mere	OE "mere"	Lake or pond, as with *Buttermere*.
moor	ON "mor"	Upland, though not usually mountainous. As in *Little Arrow Moor*.
mire	ON "myrr"	A bog, as in *Red Mire Farm*.
moss	ON "mosi"	A bog, as in *Moss Force*.
ness	ON "nes"	Promontory, as with *Bowness*.
park	ME "park"	Originally an enclosed ground for hunting, as with *Oxen Park*.

pike	OE "pic"	Summit, as in *Scafell Pike*, highest summit in England.
rigg	ON "hrygge"	Ridge, as in *Brown Rigg*
scar	ON "sker"	Normally used for small islands (skerries) but also for crags and rock outcrops on land.
syke	OE "sic"	Small stream or ditch as with *Red Syke* farm
tarn	ON "tjorn"	Another iconic Cumbrian name. Describes mountain lakes or ponds, as with *Sprinkling Tarn*.
...thwaite	ON "þveit"	The commonest single name element in the Lake District. Describes land which has been cleared of forest, as with *Braithwaite*.
tod(d)	OE	Meaning "fox" as in *Todd Crag* and *Tod Gill*.

In the explanation of place names, the following code is employed:

B	British/Brythonic
C	Cumbric (the local version of Brythonic)
OE	Old English (Anglo-Saxon)
ON	Old Norse
OFr	Old French
ME	Middle English

RIVERS AND LAKES
Aira Beck
"Aira" ON, the "gravel delta" where a stream enters a lake. **"Beck"** from ON "stream". Means "the river with the stony delta".

Aira Beck delta

Aik Beck
"Aik" ON, meaning "oak", and **"beck"** ON, "stream". The "stream where oak trees are found".
Aira Force ON, "the waterfall on Aira beck".
Angle Tarn ON, "a good fishing pond", possibly also OE influence, as words for fishing hooks are similar in each.

MOUNTAINS, FELLS AND VALLEYS
Aaron Crags
"Aaron" OE, meaning "eagle". **"Crag"** from B or ON meaning "cliff". "The cliffs where one finds eagles".

Arnison Crag
Scholars are undecided on the meaning of "Arnison", suggesting a surname, the forename Ann, or OE for "eagle", plus B/G for "cliff". Take your pick. Many names have meanings lost in the past.
Allerdale
"Aller.." from the B river name "Ellen",

unknown meaning, and **"..dale"** ON, "valley". "The valley of the River Ellen".
Ashgill Beck
"Ash" ON, for "ash trees". **"...gill"** ON, "deep valley or gorge". **"Beck"** ON, "stream". Meaning "the stream in the deep valley where there are ash trees".
Ashness
"Ash" ON, and **"..ness"**, meaning "headland". "The headland or promontory where there are ash trees".
Auterstone
This name may come from OE describing a crag which resembles an "altar".

Ash tree seeds - places are often named after plants

TOWNS, VILLAGES, FARMS, AREAS.
Abbey Flatts
"Abbey" OFr, "abbey" and **"Flatts"** ON, "level ground". Meaning "the level ground of the abbey".
Addyfield
"Addy" OE, diminutive of Adam, and **"..field"** OE, "a field belonging to someone called Adam".
Ambleside
"Amble" from a person's name. **..**"side" ON word for "shieling or summer pasture". Meaning "the shieling or summer pasture" of someone called

"Amelr", ON. It is thought that Ambleside, now one of the major centres in the Lake District, was originally perhaps a summer settlement of folk who came from somewhere larger.

Bridge House, Ambleside

Applethwaite
"Apple" OE or ON plus "**..thwaite"** ON for "clearing". Meaning "the clearing with the apple trees" Crab apples were native to the area.
Appletree Worth
Both from OE, meaning the "enclosure where you find apple trees".

Armathwaite Hall

Armathwaite Hall
"Arma.." from a word in either OFr or ME meaning "hermit" and "**...thwaite"** ON, meaning "clearing" plus **"Hall"** ME, originally a big house or mansion. Meaning "the mansion in the clearing of the hermit".
Askham
"Ask.." from ON "ash" and "**..ham"**, ON "place" "The place of the ash trees", now a village.
Aynsome
Describing the "sole house" in the area.

NAMES BEGINNING WITH "B"

RIVERS AND LAKES
Bassenthwaite
"Bassen..." from a ME or OFr personal name. "**...thwaite"** from ON meaning "clearing". Originally "the clearing of Bastun".

Rusty old signpost to Bassenthwaite

Black Syke
"Syke" is an OE word describing a stream which is slow moving, more like a ditch. Means "the dark, slow-moving stream".
Bleaberry Tarn
"Tarn" is ON for a small mountain lake. At Bleaberry Tarn you can still expect to find blaeberries in late summer.

Blea Tarn
"**Blea**" Tarn has nothing to do with blaeberries, but is derived from ON meaning "dark". So it means "the dark mountain lake".

Brathay
"**Brathay**" ON for "wide river"

Buttermere
"**Butter..**" from OE for "butter" and "**...mere**" OE for lake. Probably "the lake with good grazing for milk cows".

"The lake with good grazing for milk cows"

MOUNTAINS, FELLS AND VALLEYS

Backbarrow
"**Back..**" from OE "shaped like a back". "**..barrow**" from OE "A hill". Meaning "A back-shaped hill".

Bald Howe
A problematic name. "**Howe**" ON is clear enough, meaning one or other form of "hill". However "**Bald**" has been variously spelled over time, and it may mean "bald" or "boat-shaped" or something entirely different.

Bald Mire
"**Bald**" meaning "**bare**" ME. "**Mire**" ON meaning "marsh", presumably a "marsh devoid of trees".

Bannerdale
"**Banner..**" ON meaning "holly"; "**..dale**" ON meaning "valley". "The

valley where you find holly".

Bannerdale - after Old Norse for "holly"

Banner Rigg
Seems to suggest something like "Holly ridge", but the meaning is possibly different. "**Rigg**" ON may be "ridge", but "**Banner**" is most likely to refer to some form of boundary, implying "boundary ridge", though this is not certain.

Bassenfell
Suggested that this name is a very modern invention, using "**fell**", along with an element from nearby Bassenthwaite village.

Baystones
From OE, denoting the location where you can find the large, flat stones formerly used in baking.

Bell Rib
"**Bell**" from French "beautiful" and OE "**Rib**", somehow referring to the shape of this particular summit.

Bennethead
"**Bennet**" from ON for "holly" and "**...head**", OE for "highest point", meaning "the highest point where holly grows"

Binsey
"**Bin..**" possibly ON for "heap" (same as coal bing), plus "**..sey**", from ON "hill". Meaning "hill in the shape of a mound".

Birdhow

"Bird" from OE, referring to "birds" and ON for "hill". Clearly a hill where there were lots of birds.

Birk Crag

The "rocky cliff where you find birch trees".

Birk Moss

Similarly "the bog or marsh where there are birch trees", a description which must have applied to much of the land 1000 years ago.

Places are often named after birches (birks)

Bishop, The

A white-washed rock above Bassenthwaite which supposedly commemorates the death of the bishop-elect of Derry in 1783, trying to ride to the top of Barf hill for a wager.

Black Combe

A possible source of confusion.

"Combe" from B refers to" a valley or a corrie", whereas "**Combe**" derived from

ON refers to "a ridge" or "a crest". Black Combe is the latter, meaning "a dark coloured mountain".

The Bishop

Black Sail Pass

From ON, describing a place which was "dark and boggy", plus "**pass**".

Blencathra

"Blen..." B, refers to a summit, and "**....cathra**" a chair or saddle shape. "The chair-shaped summit". B(Cumbric)

The chair-shaped Blencathra

Blennerhazel

A modern name concocted by the family Coalbank, originally from Blennerhasset, just north of the National Park.

Blowick

From ON. "**Blow...**"meaning "dark" and

"**...wick**" describing a "bay" .

Bogle Crag

"**Bogle**" is a dialect word, also used in Scots for "phantom or ghost". "**Crag**" may have various origins (ME, G, ON) but it is now one of the iconic Lakeland words, meaning "rocky cliff". In this case perhaps "the haunted cliffs".

Borrowdale

The valley which contains and runs south from Derwentwater. From "**...dale**" ON, meaning "valley" and a tribal name," **Borgara**". The "valley of the Borgara". Alternatively it may refer to a hill fort, and may be the "valley of the fortified place".

Derwentwater from Borrowdale

Bowder Stone

Probably a Cumbrian dialect version of the word "boulder". The Bowder stone is an enormous boulder in Borrowdale, and is reputed to be one of the largest glacial erratics in Britain. Geological opinion identifies it with the fine-grained lavas on the crags above, suggesting it fell to the valley floor towards the end of the last ice age.

Brack Barrow

Possibly from OE, the "hill where you find badgers".

Bracken Rigg

"**Bracken**" originally ME, and "**Rigg**"

ON meaning "ridge". "The bracken-covered ridge".

The most visited boulder in the Lake District

Brackenthwaite

"**Bracken..**" OE "bracken", and "**...thwaite**" ON "clearing". "The clearing where there is bracken". Now a village, which is part of Buttermere.

Braithwaite

"**Brai...**" From ON meaning "broad" and "**...thwaite**", "clearing". Meaning "the broad clearing".

The beck at Braithwaite

Bram Crag

"**Bram**" possibly OE or ME referring to either "broom" or "brambles", plus "**Crag**". "The crag where brambles or broom grow".

Brandelhow

"**Brandel..**" is probably derived from

the personal name "Brandulf". "**...how**" is from ON for "hill". Originally meaning "the hill of Brandulf".
Brandreth
Possibly from ON, describing it's function as a beacon hill".

TOWNS, VILLAGES AND AREAS
Bandrake Head
From ON, possibly describing the "protruding ridge". "**Head**" refers to the elevated position of the present houses on the ridge.
Bank Ground
"**Bank**" a family name, and "**Ground**" referring to the family land or farm. ME "The Bank family farm".
Barkbooth
Several names contain the element "**bark**" from ON, which refers to a bark industry, producing tannine for leather making. In this instance the name probably describes a building where bark was dried or processed.
Barton
From OE, meaning "barley-growing farm".
Bateman Fold ME meaning "the enclosure" or maybe just the "farm of the Batemans".
Beckcote Farm
"**Beck**" ON for stream. "**Cote**" OE for cottage, with modern English "**farm**". Meaning "the farm named after the cottage beside the stream".

"The bottom of the stream"

Beckfoot and **Beck Head**
"**Beck**" ON for "stream" with the modern English meaning the "bottom of the stream" and the "top of the stream", respectively.
Bethecar
From ON, the "shieling or summer pasture of Bethoc or Bethog".
Bield
Meaning "shelter or lair".
Birkby
A nice example of a name which seems to have one meaning, but in fact has something quite different. One might expect something to do with "birch trees", but the earliest spellings suggest an ON meaning of "the village of the British". Diana Whaley comments on the importance of this name, in that it provides evidence of the survival of a distinctive Brythonic-speaking community in southwest Cumbria, well after the arrival of the Vikings.
Blawith
ON, meaning "the dark forest"
Bleathwaite
"**Blea..**" ON meaning "dark"
"**...thwaite**" ON meaning "clearing".
"The dark clearing".
Boot
Derived from ME, "bend" most likely in the valley.

Boot Village

18

Bootle
OE refers to a "building".

Borrans
OE referring to a " burial cairn".

Bowness
The Ennerdale version derives from OE word for "bow" or "curved", plus (OE) or ON "**..ness**" meaning a promontory or headland. Meaning "the curved headland".

Bowness-on-Windermere
This has a different derivation and meaning. "**Bow..**" came from an OE word for "bull". "**...ness**" comes from OE for promontory or headland, giving an initial meaning of "the promontory where the bull (probably a communal bull) was kept". For Windermere, see page 53.

The boatyard at Bowness-on-Windermere

Brantwood
Probably ME meaning "burnt wood". Southern Lakeland was well-known for charcoal burning.

Bridge End
There are many names which include the element bridge, almost all of which can be taken at face-value.

Brigham
"**Brig...**" ON meaning "bridge" or "quayside". "**...ham** " derived from ON and OE for a piece of land beside water.

Brockhole
National Park Information Centre. From OE meaning the "badger's sett or hole".

Popular Visitor Centre near Ambleside

Broom, The
"**Broom**" occurs in several names, and relates to the evergreen and golden flowered shrub.

Broughton
"**Brough...**" OE meaning stream, and "**...ton**", OE meaning village or some form of settlement. Now "the village beside the stream".

Brow
ME Cumbrian word meaning **"slope"**.

Brundholme
"**Brund...**" Mixture of ME or ON meaning **"burned"** and "**...holme**", ON referring to land beside the water. "The burned land beside the water".

Butterwick
From OE meaning "the dairy farm".

Byrestead
From OE, "the farm with some sort of a building", not necessarily what we now know as a byre.

Names beginning with C

RIVERS AND LAKES

Cocker
The name of the river draining from Crummock Water to Cockermouth. From the B meaning "crooked".

Coniston
The name of the Lake and the village. Believed to be of the same origin as the various "Kingston" names throughout England, meaning "the king's village or estate"

Pier on Lake Coniston

Crake River
From the B (Cumbric) for "rocky". The "rocky river".

Crummock Water
Refers to something "crooked" or "with bends". Maybe the river; perhaps the lake itself. Lakes are almost never called "lake", but usually "mere" or "water".

MOUNTAINS, FELLS AND VALLEYS

Caer Mote
There is debate about this name, which is probably Cumbric, but it is possible that **"Caer"** relates to a "fortified hill" and **"Mote"** to a "meeting place".

Calva, Great
From ON, the "calf hill" or "hill where calves have their pasture".

Canny Hill
Hill named after a family called Canny or Kanny.

Capell Crag
"Capell" derives from ME for "horse" and **"Crag"**, from various possible sources meaning "rocky cliff".

Carling Knott
From ON word for **"witch"**, plus **"Knott"** ON meaning "rocky hill." Could be the "witches' hill".

Carrock Fell
Same derivation as **"Cark"**, meaning "rock" or "rocky", together with **"Fell"**, ON meaning "mountain". "The rocky mountain".

Castle Rock
A pile of rocks in St John's in the Vale, which resembles a castle.

Castle How
Modern English **"Castle"**, with **"How"** ON meaning "fortified hill" or "hill with a castle or fort".

Castlerigg
Presently best known for the famous stone circle. Means "the fortified ridge", or "ridge with a fort".

Castlerigg Stone Circle, near Keswick

Catbells
The well-known and prominent hill west of Derwentwater. Modern name denoting the "bell-shaped hills where one finds wild cats".

Catbells

Cat Bields
The den of the wild cat.

Chapel Stile
Can be taken at face value, meaning the "stile into the chapel".

Clough Head
"Clough" from OE meaning "gorge" or "ravine", plus "Head" meaning the "head of". The "head of the gorge".

Cofa Pike
"Cofa" is probably OE referring to the "corrie" below the "Pike", ON for "peak or pointed hill".

Coledale
"Cole..." probably derives from ON, referring to "charcoal burning" and "...dale" is ON for "valley. "The charcoal burning valley".

Common Fell
The mountain which is common land, with grazing and other rights.

Crag
"Crag" occurs in Lake District names several hundred times. Whaley suggests the origins are Gaelic, but that the word was brought from Gaelic-speaking areas by Norse invaders. Usually describes a rocky outcrop on a mountain, but may also refer to lesser rock exposures.

Cuckoo Brow
"Brow" meaning slope, and "Cuckoo" is self-explanatory. The author has experienced numerous places with a preponderance of cuckoos, and this could have been one of them.

TOWNS, VILLAGES AND AREAS.
Caldbeck
"Cald..." Probably from OE meaning "cold" and "...beck" ON, meaning "stream". "The cold stream". It is not likely that this beck was colder than any other, but likely someone thought so.

A rusty old road sign

Calgarth
"Cal..."from ON or OE for "calf" and "...garth" ON for "an enclosure or field". Literally "the calf's field"

Cark
As in Cark-in-Cartmel. Some debate here. Possible B (Cumbric), meaning "rock", but also possible is a derivation from a word for "stream".

Cockenskell
"Cocken..." derives from a family name "Cocken" and "...skell" relates to the ON word meaning "summer pasture" or "shieling". "The summer pasture of the Cocken family".

Cockermouth
Where the River Cocker joins the River Derwent.

Cocklaw Fell
Refers to the existence of black grouse (Blackcocks) and their fascinating display habits, in which the males perform on a regular site called a "lek". "**Cock..**" comes from OE, and "**...law**" from ON for "play", and "**Fell**" is ON for "mountain". "The mountain where the black grouse display", a lovely name.

Cockpit
The stone circle on Divock Moor, southwest of the village of Askham. The name is modern, probably a misinterpretation of the original function of the stone circle. It is unlikely it was ever used as a cockpit.

Copstone near the Cockpit on Moor Divock

Copstone
Possibly OE meaning "summit stone".

Cowmire Hall
Fairly self-explanatory. "The marshy place where the cows (or calves) have their pasture", plus "**Hall**", originally being a big house or mansion.

Croft Head
"**Croft**" is most likely from OE, although

the word is still commonly used in Gaelic. It refers to a small piece of land, specifically smaller than the normal farm enclosure. The "top of the small enclosure".

Crook
From the ON, referring to "the bend in the river".

Crookdale
"**Crook..**" from ON for "bend", and "**..dale**" ON for "valley. "The crooked valley".

Aerial view of The Cockpit on Moor Divock

Numerous places have the word "**cross**" in their name. Most refer to an association with a Christian cross; some are at cross-roads.

Cumbria
Orginally from OE word meaning "the land of the Cwmry", the so-called Brythonic Celts who occupied this area, together with southern Scotland, as the Romans invaded.

Cunswick
"**Cun...**" from ON, meaning the "king" and "**...wick**", a "farm " or "settlement". Most likely the "king's farm".

RIVERS AND LAKES

Deep Gill
Modern English "deep" together with "**Gill**" ON meaning "the deep ravine".

Derwentwater
The name of the lake on which Keswick stands, plus the river which flows from it. An ancient Brythonic name believed to describe "a river with oak trees along its banks"

Derwentwater Landings

Derwentfolds
"**Derwent...**" plus "**...folds**" common OE word meaning "enclosure".

Dob Gill
"**Dob**" probably comes from the still used Cumbrian word "dub" meaning "pool". So the meaning is "the ravine with a pool or pools".

Dock Tarn
Most likely the "mountain pool with water lilies". OE and ON.

Duddon
River and valley name. One of the names where there is no clear meaning. Certainly old, with the first written evidence in the 12th century. Possibly a personal name.

Dungeon Ghyll Force
Dungeon OF referring to a "cavern or prison" ; "**Ghyll**" ON, reinforcing the description of a "ravine" and "**Force**" from ON for "waterfall". "The waterfall in the cavern-like ravine".

MOUNTAINS, FELLS AND VALLEYS

Dale
"**Dale**" ON, one of the commonest names in the Lake District, means "valley". Added to it are modern English words describing various parts of the valley, all fairly self-explanatory: Dale Bottom, Dale End, Dale Foot etc.

Dockray
Probably ON, meaning a "hollow".

Dodd
The name occurs on many occasions and appears to describe a particular form of hill. Probably ME, the name usually describes a steep hill, with a rounded summit.

Sign on the western slopes of Skiddaw

Dollywaggon Pike
An unusual and attractive name, with the earliest written record in the 19th century, so probably recent, though not necessarily. "**Dolly...**" may be derived

from a personal name or from the carts called "dollies" used in mining. It is uncertain. **"Pike"** is a summit.

Dryhowe
A mixture of OE and ON, meaning "dry hill", in the sense of not being marshy.

Dubwath
"Dub..." derives from ON for "pool" and **"...wath"** probably ON, referring to a "secluded spot". The "pool at the secluded spot".

Dunmail Raise
The pass between Grasmere and Thirlmere-St Johns in the Vale. **"Dunmail"** refers to a 10th century Cumbrian king. **"Raise"**, ON for "burial cairn". The cairn also marked an important historical political boundary.

Dunnerdale
There is some debate, but probably meaning "the valley of the river Duddon".

TOWNS, VILLAGES AND AREAS
Dacre
An old name from C, meaning "trickling", refers to the small stream which gave the village of Dacre its name.

Dalegarth
"Dale..." ON "valley", plus **"... garth"** ON meaning an "enclosure" or simply "farm". "The farm in the valley".

Dalemain

Dalemain
The mansion between Penrith and Ullswater. **"Dale.."** plus an ON or G family or personal name, meaning "the valley of someone called Mani".

Deer Bields
"Bield" is an ON word for "the place where animals stay or hide". **"Deer"** is from OE with the modern meaning.

Deer Rudding
"Rudding" is derived from an OE word meaning "clearing". "The clearing where there were deer".

Dove Cottage
Dove Cottage, home of the poet William Wordsworth, is the most famous house in the Lake District During Wordsworth's time the house apparently did not have a name. "Dove Cottage" was only used 80 years after his death.

Dove Cottage

Drigg
Probably from an ON word meaning to "drag". Whether this was boats, some form of cargo, or even fish is unknown.

Dub How Farm
"Dub" ON meaning "pool"; **"How"** from ON meaning "hill", plus farm. "The farm beside the hill with a pond".

LAKES AND RIVERS

Eamont

From OE words meaning "river" and "meet". The "river confluence". The village of Eamont lies between the rivers Eamont and Lowther. Diana Whaley suggests that the place was named before the river.

Eamont Bridge near Penrith

Ellen, River

Flows from near Ireby to enter the sea at Maryport. As with many river names, Ellen is thought to be ancient. Most likely a Brit word, with unsubstantiated speculation of a meaning like "mighty", "strong" or "holy".

Ellerbeck

"**Eller...**" ON refers to "alder trees", which grow in wet areas. "**...beck**" ON

Upper Eskdale

for stream. The "stream with alders".

Esk, River

"**Esk**" is likely to have derived from a Cumbric word simply meaning "water" or "river". So the meaning today could simply be "river river" or "river of water". Believed to be the same B derivation as Exe, Axe and Esk, which are found in many parts of Britain.

MOUNTAINS, FELLS AND VALLEYS

Eagle Crag

"**Eagle**" from ME, meaning a bird of prey, probably a golden eagle, and "**Crag**" from G, " cliff". "The cliff where the golden eagles are". Some suggest "sea eagles" rather than golden eagles.

Ecclerigg

"**Eccle...**" possibly derives from the latinisation of a Brit word meaning "church", plus "**...rigg**" , meaning "ridge". The "ridge by the church".

Eel Crag

According to most commentators unlikely to be derived from the marine creature, the eel, but probably from the word "ill" , referring to the rugged nature of the rocky cliffs.

Elfhowe

"**Elf...**" likely from OE, referring to the "little people" or "fairies". "**...how**" is derived from ON, meaning "hill". There was a general belief in supernatural beings and superstitions in many areas of Britain, especially mountainous regions, continuing even today.

Elmhow

Names referring to trees are common, with "**Elm...**" suggesting a place with elm trees and "**...how**" ON, meaning "hill". The "hill where elm trees grow".

TOWNS, VILLAGES AND AREAS
Easthwaite
"Eas.." derived for the ON word for "east", plus **"...thwaite"** from ON for "clearing". The "easternmost clearing".
Elva Plain
The location of a formerly-impressive stone circle. **"Elva"** is probably derived from OE for "elf" or "fairy", resulting from the belief that the circle was associated with some supernatural or spiritual activity. Plus **"plain"**, although the site is more of a south-facing slope than a plain.

Access the stone circle through this farm

NAMES BEGINNING WITH "F"

LAKES AND STREAMS
Flass
Originally from ON meaning "swamp".
Foutern Tarn
A small lake, the meaning of which is unknown.
Force
"Fors" from ON, fairly common term for "waterfall". Best known is probably Aira Force.

Converted mill named after a local waterfall

Embleton
Probably from ON, meaning the "settlement of Eanbald".
Ennerdale
From a personal name, plus **"...dale"** ON, meaning "valley". "Anund's valley".
Eskdale
Some commentators suggest that the name of the valley was derived from "ash trees" ON, rather than simply "the valley of the river Esk".

Foulsyke
A name found in various places in Cumbria. **"...syke"** normally refers to "a slow-moving stream" as opposed to a mountain stream.

MOUNTAINS, FELLS AND VALLEYS
Fair Rigg
"Fair" from the OE meaning "fine" or "lovely", and **"Rigg"** from the ON word meaning "ridge". The "fine ridge".
Falcon Crag
It is suggested that Falcon Crag in Borrowdale was a haunt of peregrines.
Foule Crag
Two possible OE meanings, one relates to "birds", the other a "foul rocky cliff" in a modern sense, suggesting that it is

"dangerous". Either the "rocky cliff with birds" or "dangerous crag".

Fox Ghyll
"The stream or gorge where you get foxes".

Friar's Crag
On Derwentwater, one of the Lake District's most photographed locations. Originally from OFr, referring to a member of a monastic order, a **"Friar"**, and **"Crag"**, meaning a "rocky outcrop" beside the lake. Local folklore suggests an association with St Herbert.

Fusedale
From ON, the "valley with the byre".

Friar's Crag overlooking Derwentwater

"the felled trees" and **"Park"** meaning "a field or hunting enclosure".

Fellborough
Seems like the name of a settlement, but probably originally described the hilly land west of Windermere, although the word **"fell"** would not normally be used for land of such low altitude. One of many names which remain unclear as to their origin.

Felldyke
Probably denotes the "head-dyke" or "head-wall" which separates the improved "in-by" land in the valley, from the unimproved fell of the high ground.

Fenwick
"Fen..." is likely from OE "marsh", together with **"...wick"** OE meaning "place " or "settlement". The "place beside the marsh".

Ferney Green
Uncertain origin, but may be the "pasture of the Furnell family".

Finsthwaite
"Finn's clearing", from ON personal name and **"...thwaite"**, for "clearing".

TOWNS, VILLAGES AND AREAS
Far Sawrey
"Sawrey" is believed to be from an ON word meaning "damp" or "dirty", perhaps describing the boggy land west of Windermere. **"Far"** seems recent, relating to the division of the Sawrey estate into "Near" and Far".

Farthwaite
"Far..." Probably the "furthermost" and **"...thwaite"** ON, meaning "clearing". The "furthermost clearing".

Fawe Park
"Fawe" is probably from OE, meaning

Finsthwaite Church

Fisherground Farm
Refers to the "farm belonging to the Fisher family". **"Farm"** is a recent addition repeating the meaning.

Floshgate
Most likely the "gate to the lake" (to Ullswater in this case") from a ME word meaning pool or marsh.

Fold Gate
The reason for this name is uncertain. From original spellings it did not refer to a fold, ie an enclosure, but a "foul gate". Perhaps the gate into a place that was considered dirty or unclean.

Frith Wood
"**Frith**" is believed to derive from OE, meaning "wood". As with many names, the different elements merely repeat the meaning.

A busy market town in south Lakeland

Furness
A name which causes some debate. Joan Lee suggests "the further promontory or headland". Diana Whaley seems to favour "headland beside the island called **"Fuo"**.

NAMES BEGINNING WITH "G"

RIVERS AND LAKES
Galesyke
"**...syke**" refers to a relatively sluggish stream, slow flowing. "**Gale...**" is believed to be a name for the shrub "bog-myrtle". The "slow stream where myrtle is found".

Ghyll (Gill)
From the ON describing a "narrow, ravine-like valley with a stream". There are many examples.

Gill Force
From ON, meaning the "waterfall in the ravine or gash in the hillside".

Gilpin, River
After a prominent Westmorland family.

Goats Water
Wild goats are still common in Scotland and also in Snowdonia, but this little lake near Coniston is thought to have been one of their last refuges in the Lake District. They were common since Neolithic times, about 5000 years ago.

Gowan, River
Believed to have been extrapolated from the Gowan Bridge, thought to have come from an ON personal name or possibly the name for "daisy".

Grasmere
Lake and Village. Probably from OE, the "lake surrounded by grass".

Reflections on Grasmere

Greta, River
The River Greta joins the Derwent near Keswick. It's name is found in several Norse-speaking lands, and means "rocky", The "rocky river".

Grizebeck
From ON meaning "pigs" and **"...beck"** meaning "stream". The "stream where pigs are kept".

MOUNTAINS, FELLS AND VALLEYS
Gap, The
The word gap refers to a col or a pass. Usually it is qualified, as with "Windy Gap".

Gatesgarthdale
A complicated name deriving from a number of ON words. "**Gate...**" refers to "goats", "**...sgarth...**" derives from a word meaning "pass" and "**...dale**" describes a "valley". Probably the "valley at the foot of the pass frequented by goats".

Glaramara
The meaning of Glaramara, the mountain at the southern end of Borrowdale is unclear, and a matter of debate amongst academics. Probably coming from ON, referring to "summer pastures" and "ravines" but by no means certain.

One of the Lake District's outdoor centres

Glen
"Glen" most likely derives from Gaelic or Cumbric meaning "valley", usually a "mountain valley" as opposed to a "lowland valley". However, an ON origin is also possible, meaning "open place amongst the rocks"

Glencoyne
"Glen..." almost certainly meaning "valley" probably from C. However the "**...coyne**" element causes some debate, with suggestions ranging from "reedy" to "beautiful" depending on the interpretation of the evidence.

Glencoyne

Gouther Crag
Possibly relating to the echo achievable at the crags. Probably literally meaning "barking rocks", but more likely "cliffs which echo".

Great Dodd
The word **"great"** appears frequently as an element in Lake District names. Usually it simply means "large", and is often used as a comparative name, ie the "larger" of two or more. Great Dodd is simply the "large rounded hill".

Great Gable
"Gable" from ON, refers to the gable (end of a house) or angular shape of

the mountain. **"Great"** is simply "large".

Graystones

Though **"Gray…"** appears in numerous names, meaning the colour "grey", in this case Graystones is likely to refer specifically to "boundary stones".

Greenburn

The word green occurs very frequently, along with various other colours, and suggests the awareness of the early clearers of the land of the different shades of the landscape.

There are green crags, burns, dales, farms, holes, holmes and howes, as well as numerous others. Generally the names derive from ON, simply meaning "green" and they may originally have referred to either the freshness and colour of the land or maybe simply to "grass".

TOWNS, VILLAGES AND AREAS

Galava

The name describes a Roman Fort in Ambleside, thought to be of B origin, and of unknown meaning.

Sign in Ambleside using the Roman name

Gaitscale

From ON, the "shieling" or "summer pasture" where there are goats.

Garnett Bridge

Bridge named after a local family who were called Garnett.

Garth Heads

"Garth" meaning farm or enclosure. **"Heads"** referring to the top or higher end of a farm.

Gillerthwaite

Diana Whaley describes this as a problem name, perhaps "the clearing with the streams", or possibly relating to "snares". All from ON.

Glenridding pier, Ullswater

Glenridding

"Glen…" almost certainly derives from either Cumbric or G, meaning "valley", usually a "mountain valley". The **"…ridding"** element may be from ME, meaning "clearing" or it may come from a Cumbric word referring to "bracken". Either the "valley with the clearing" or the "valley with bracken".

Grange

In most cases **"grange"** will be derived from OFr and/or ME and will refer to a farm which is remote from the main farm.

Grisedale

"Grise..." from ON refers to "pigs", and may have been associated with "pasturing" pigs on acorns. **"...dale"** also ON, is a "valley". The "valley where pigs pasture". Grisedale, with the Forestry Commission since 1934, is one of Lakeland's largest forests.

NAMES BEGINNING WITH "H"

RIVERS AND LAKES

Hare Gill
"Hare" most likely the name of the animal. **"Gill"** from ON meaning "ravine or gorge", though it is also often used for the "stream" itself.

Haweswater
"Haw..." likely refers to a ON personal name, with **"...water"** describing a "lake".

Hell Gill
"Gill..." from ON meaning "ravine", sometimes referring to the "stream in a ravine". **"Hell..."** possibly referring to " a cave-like ravine".

High Force
The falls upstream of Aira Force. **"Force"** derives from ON for "waterfall" and **"High"** has its modern meaning. The "high" or perhaps "higher waterfall".

MOUNTAINS, FELLS AND VALLEYS

Haltcliff
"Halt..." first appeared in the 13th century and is derived from OFr , meaning "high". The element **"..cliff"** initially referred to a "ravine".

Hard Knott
Derived from ON, literally meaning "hard" and **"Knott"**, also ON, meaning

a "rocky summit".

Hart Crag
"Hart" probably from OE referring to "deer", and **"Crag"** referring to a "rocky cliff".
The "rocky cliff where you find deer".

Hartsop
"Hart..." OE for "deer". **"...sop"**, likely OE referring to a "valley". The "valley where deer are found".

Places are often named after animals

Haverigg
"Haver..." is from ON, meaning "oats" **"...rigg"** from ON, meaning "ridge". The "ridge where oats grow".
The author recalls the word "haver" still being used for "oats" during his childhood in north Cumbria, usually in the form of "mashed haver", meaning bruised oats for fodder.

Haycock
Combination of OE words for "hay" and for "heap". A hill resembling a "pile of hay".

Haystack
"Haystack" is still the Cumbrian word for a "hay rick" and likely derives from ON. The name presumably means "resembling hay ricks".

Hegdale
"Heg..." is probably derived from ON for the wild "Bird Cherry", *Prunus*

"padus. "**...dale**" from ON meaning "valley". The "valley where you find Bird Cherries".

Helm Crag
Possibly from an ON word referring to a "helmet shape".

Helvellyn
One of Lakeland's four 3000 foot summits, but there is no agreement on the meaning of the name. It may derive from Cumbric meaning "yellow upland" or possibly comes from a Cumbric word simply meaning "mountain" or "hill".

Helvellyn from Thirlmere

steeper than surrounding hills High Stile is the "high and steep" hill between Buttermere and Ennerdale.

Honister Pass
Diana Whaley describes Honister as " a good example of the frustration arising from the lack of early evidence". The best guess is that "**Honi...**" derives from an ON personal name, and "**...ster**" also comes from ON, meaning a "farm-stead", though there is also the possibility of it referring to a "summer pasture" or "shieling".

Honister slate mine on Honister Pass

High Pike
"**Pike**" from ON meaning "summit". "**High**" differentiating between two summits.

High Scarth Crag
"**Crag**" refers to a "rocky exposure", and "**Scarth**", from ON meaning a "pass" or "col". The "crag next to the high pass".

High Spy
Though probably from OFr, the name can likely be taken fairly literally, meaning the "high place where you can spy from" , or a "high look-out place".

High Stile
"**Stile**" probably derives from OE meaning "steep". Though not any

How(e)
ON, usually referring to a "hill", as opposed to a mountain or fell. There are many examples.

TOWNS, VILLAGES AND AREAS
Hag End
"**Hag**" is thought to be ON, meaning an "area of felled trees". "**End**" has its normally modern meaning. The "end of the felled area".

Halecat
A name with various possible mean-ings. Diana Whaley suggests that "**...cat**" may refer either to the "wild cat" or it may relate to an ON personal

name. **"Hale..."** may refer to an isolated piece of land, or even a "cat's tail". Take your pick.

Hannakin
Probably one of frequent examples where a name is derived from a diminutive, in this case probably **"Annikin"**, from the original "Ann", most likely the daughter of a former occupant, Richard Ashburner.

Haverthwaite
"Haver..." ON, referring to "oats". **"...thwaite"** ON for "clearing". The "clearing where oats are grown".

Hawkshead
The village west of Windermere. The element" **Hawk..."** is likely a personal name, and the 12-13th century name described a "summer pasture or shieling". It seems that about 100 years after the first written record of the name, it was changed to its present form, probably referring to a "hill".

Herdwick
Although the name Herdwick now describes the hardy breed of Lakeland sheep, it originally came from an OE word for a "grazing" or "pasture farm" as opposed to an "arable farm". In the Lake District herdwicks were grazing units of land under one shepherd.

The Herdwick breed of sheep

High Street
A combination of OE and Latin, referring to the Roman road crossing the high moors from Windermere north-eastwards towards Penrith.

Hobkin Ground
The "land or farm belonging to the Hobkin family".

Hollens Farm
There are numerous names including Hollen(s) or Hollin(s), meaning "holly", derived from OE. Hollens Farm means Holly Farm, and there are many other names of features and places identifying with the holly found there.

This name derives from "holly"

Hospital Plantation
At one time sufferers from highly infectious diseases ended up very much in isolation, well away from centres of population. The Lake District itself had several of these "isolation hospitals". The woodland on Whinlatter Pass had one such place.

Hundreds, The
Divisions of the common grazing before the land was enclosed.

NAMES BEGINNING WITH "I"

LAKES, RIVERS AND WATER
Ing Bridge
"**Ing**" is ON for "meadow". The "bridge next to the meadow".
Irt , River
One of the names where the meaning is unknown. As with most rivers, the name is likely to be ancient, probably Brythonic.

MOUNTAINS, FELLS AND VALLEYS
Idle Hill
Hill with connections to a family called Idle.
Iving Howe
"**Iving**" is derived from ON, meaning "ivy", plus "**Howe**", ON meaning "hill". The "hill where you find ivy".

TOWNS, VILLAGES AND AREAS.
Ickenthwaite
Unusual name with a quaint meaning. "**Icken...**" derives from an ON word for "squirrels". "**...thwaite**" refers to a "clearing". So the name means the "clearing where there are squirrels". Obviously this would have referred to the native red squirrel.

Farm buildings at Ickenthwaite

Intack, High
From ON, describing the formerly open land which was enclosed. "**High Intack**" refers to an enclosure high on the fell.
Irton
An OE name meaning the "settlement on the river Irt". But there is no clear idea as to the meaning of "**Irt**".

Ickenthwaite - "where there are squirrels"

THERE ARE VERY FEW PLACE NAMES IN THE LAKE DISTRICT WHICH BEGIN WITH "J", ALMOST ALL INVOLVE PERSONAL NAMES.

NAMES BEGINNING WITH "K"

LAKES AND RIVERS
Kent, river
Kent is an old B name, the meaning of which is lost.
Kentmere
"**Kent**", the river, and "**...mere**", OE for "lake" or "tarn". The "tarn beside the river Kent".

The river Kent at Kendal

especially oats, prior to milling. Kilns used for pottery were rare.

Kiln Bank
The "slope beside the kiln".

Kilnstones
The "stony place beside the kiln".

Kirkbank
"**Kirk…**" commonly derived from ON, meaning "church", though Joan Lee cites numerous examples which possibly come from OE or OF meaning "circle", suggesting the importance of stone circles in some names, many now disappeared. Most likely the "slope beside the church".

Kirk Fell
Joan Allen again feels this name is more likely to come from OE, referring to the "circular shape" of the mountain, rather than a church.

MOUNTAINS, FELLS AND VALLEYS

Kelbarrow
"**Kel…**" from ON meaning "spring" ie the start of a stream, and "**…barrow**", meaning "hill". The "hill where there is a spring".

Keppel Cove
Keppel is most likely from ME, meaning a "horse", and **Cove**, from OE, referring to a "corrie", the head of a glaciated valley, often, though not always, with a tarn. The "corrie associated with horses".

Kepple Crag
Kepple is most likely derived from ON, referring to "horses", plus **Crag**, from ON or G, meaning a "rocky place or cliff".

Kettle Crag
Kettle is probably from ON or OE meaning a "hollow". **Crag** from ON for a "rocky cliff" or "outcrop". The "cliff beside the hollow".

Kiln
Several names include the word kiln, Kilns could have served a number of purposes. Lime-kilns are very common, especially where there are outcrops of limestone. In addition, kilns were very commonly used for drying grain,

The inn at the head of Kirkstone Pass

Kirkstone Pass
Possibly refers to a particular stone which looks like a church, plus "**pass**".

Knott
"**Knott**" occurs often. It derives from ON and is usually a hill standing alone, often compact, with many of them rocky.

35

TOWNS, VILLAGES, SETTLEMENTS AND AREAS

Kelton
Many names begin with the element "**Kel**" or "**Keld**", from ON for "spring". "**...ton**" comes from OE for "farmstead" or some form of "settlement", meaning the "farmstead at the spring".

Kendal
Town named after the valley. "**Ken...**" derives from the B name of the river Kent, the meaning of which is lost. "**...dal**" is from ON for "valley". The "valley of the river Kent".

Keswick
Lakeland's biggest town and the centre of the northern lakes tourist industry. Most likely from OE, describing a "dairy farm which makes cheese".

Keswick's busy town centre

Kirklands
From ON "**Kirk..**" meaning "church". "The lands which belonged to the church".

Kirkthwaite
"**Kirk...**" ON meaning "church" and "**...thwaite**", a "clearing". The "clearing with a church".

Knipe Fold
The "enclosure" OE, of the Knipe family.

NAMES BEGINNING WITH "L"

LAKES AND RIVERS

Leven, River
As with many names of rivers, "**Leven**" is likely to be extremely old, and there are various suggestions, possibly describing a "smooth river", but with little firm evidence.

Levers Water
This small lake was probably named after a personal name.

Linbeck
"**Lin...**" from ON, referring to "lime trees", and "**...beck**", "stream". The "stream with the lime trees".

Lodore
Famous falls in Borrowdale. Probably from ON for "low door", the "door" being the gorge through which the Watendlath beck flows prior to the falls.

Loweswater
"**Lowes...**" from ON meaning "leafy lake", with "**...water**", added later. Most of the lake is tree-lined.

Tree-lined Loweswater

MOUNTAINS, FELLS, AND VALLEYS

Ladies Table
Wainwright suggested this as the name for a particular flat rock, west of Bassenthwaite, on which Victorian ladies spread their picnics.

Lang How
"Lang" from ON meaning "long" and **"Howe"**, "hill". The "long hill".

Langrigg
"Lang.." from ON, simply meaning "long" and **"...rigg"**, describing a "ridge". The "long ridge".

Langdale
"Lang..." and **"..dale"**, both elements from ON, the "long valley".

Langdale Pikes
"Langdale" as above, **"Pikes"** from ON meaning "summits. "The summits at the long valley".

Langdale Pikes from Tarn Howes

Langstrath
Some commentators assume the **"...strath"** element is the G for "valley", usually a wide or lowland valley. Whaley sources early written mention of the name and identifies an ON name meaning "long marsh".

Latter Barrow
It is likely that **"Latter"** derives from ON, meaning a "shelter" or "den", plus **"Barrow"**, a "hill".

Latrigg
The 367m hill used in the annual Keswick games hill race. There is debate about the origins of the name, either from ON or G.

The inn in the "long valley"

Laverock How
"Laverock" comes from ON/OE for "lark", plus **"How"**, from ON meaning "hill". The "hill where you find larks".

Lickbarrow
"Lick..." OE referring to a "corpse". Probably literally the "hill of the dead", in other words an ancient "burial mound".

Lindale
"Lin..." from ON for "lime trees", and **"...dale"**, ON "valley". The "valley with the lime trees".

Ling Comb
"Ling" or **"lyng"** ON, are common elements referring to "heather", usually *Calluna vulgaris*, and **"Comb"**, a B word for "valley-basin", also known as a "corrie". "Corrie with the heather".

Ling Fell
ON, the "mountain with the heather".

Ling Mell
"Ling" meaning "heather", ON. **"Mell"** from B, meaning "bald" (both hills and men) The "heathery, bald hill".

Lion and the Lamb

One of Lakeland's most recognisable landmarks. When viewed from the southern end of Dunmail Raise, the rocks on the summit of Helm Crag, north of Grasmere, are said the resemble a lion and a lamb.

Loughrigg

"Lough..." from B/OE meaning "lake" and **"...rigg"**, from ON meaning "ridge". The "ridge beside the lake".

The Lion and the Lamb, near Grasmere.

TOWNS, VILLAGES AND AREAS

Laconby

"...by" derives from ON, meaning "settlement, farm or just place". The first element is most probably derived from a personal name.

Lake District

A name probably unused until the 1820s. Now , of course the name of the area and of the National Park.

Lamplugh

Whaley and other scholars lean towards a meaning from B, describing a "bare valley". However, Joan Lee gives a totally different meaning, said to derive from C, meaning "the church of the parish".

Linkeldsfield

Complicated name, including possible connotations of several meanings, all from ON. **"Lin..."** meaning "flax", **"...skeld..."** perhaps meaning "shieling", or possibly from the ON for "spring", plus the modern **"field"**. Probably the "shieling or spring where flax is grown".

Little Arrow

An example of a name which has become anglicised in its spelling over time. The meaning has nothing to do with arrows, but is probably ON, either a "little shieling" or perhaps a location on a "hill-slope" , depending on which interpretation you accept.

Littlethwaite

"...thwaite" from ON "clearing". Literally the "little clearing".

Longthwaite

The "long clearing".

Lorton

Some debate over this one. Obviously **"...ton"** derives from OE for "village" or "farmstead", although the first element **"Lor..."** is unclear. Possibly ON means "roaring", perhaps refers to the noisy, adjacent River Cocker, but not clear.

Lowther

Unclear, and there is some debate about the meaning, but possibly from ON meaning "foaming river".

Lowther Castle

LAKES AND STREAMS

Meadley
A reservoir. "**Mead...**" is probably from OE "meadow" and "**...ley**" also OE referring to a "clearing" (as usual Lake District "**thwaite**") The "clearing with the meadow".

Millbeck Farm

Millbeck
Self explanatory. The "millstream".

Mite, River
An early name describing the river as "trickling". This is especially the case during a dry summer.

Monk Foss
"**Foss**" is possibly derived from ON, meaning "waterfall", but equally likely is "ditch" from the Latin. "**Monk**" relates to Furness Abbey. Scholars suggest that the original name related to a ditch, but later acknowledged the waterfall which was also in the vicinity. The "monks' ditch or the monks' waterfall". Take your pick.

MOUNTAINS, FELLS AND VALLEYS

Mardale
"**Mar...**" from OE meaning "lake. "**...dale**" comes from ON meaning "valley". The "valley with a lake".

Mart Crag
Probably "the rocky area with pine martens".

Matterdale
The name is thought to relate to the ON name for the edible white-flowered wild plant *Galium Boreale*, or Northern Bedstraw, and "**...dale**". "The valley where the northern bedstraw grows".

MATTERDALE END

Probably after the ON plant name

Meal Fell
From Cumbric and ON, the "bald hill".

Mellbreak
There is the suggestion of an unusual Gaelic origin, meaning "dappled hill", though this is not certain.

Mickledore
Describes the great gap or col between Scafell and Scafell Pike, using the analogy of a door. "**Mickle**" from ON/OE, meaning "large", plus "**door**".

Middle Dodd
In the middle between Hartsop Dodd and High Hartsop Dodd. "**Dodd**" means a hill which is smooth and compact.

Mirehouse
"**Mire....**" Derived from ON, meaning "marshy land". The "house at or beside the marsh".

39

Mirk Howe

"Mirk", a word creeping back into our usage in weather forecasts. Originally from ON and meaning "dark" or "dull" Plus **"Howe"** meaning "hill". "Dark Hill".

Moor

Common term derived from OE, usually unimproved , infertile upland, though not high enough to be called a fell or mountain .

Moorcock Hall

Referring to a moor frequented by the male grouse. **"Hall"** normally refers to a large house or mansion, though today it is often merely a farm.

Moor Divock

Suggested that this is an old name, probably Brythonic. Diana Whaley suggests Divock comes from a personal name, possibly originally meaning "the dark one", though there is some debate. The area of Moor Divock was clearly important in the late Neolithic and Bronze ages.

Moor Divock burial cist

Mosedale

Various examples, all from ON, meaning the "boggy valley", (see **"Moss"**).

Moss

"Moss" is the name often given to a peat bog. Derives from either ON or OE.

Moss Eccles Tarn

"Tarn" derived from ON, meaning "small lake"; **"Moss"** suggesting the lake was originally a "bog" or was associated with the bog; **"Eccles"** is believed to be a personal name.

Muncaster

...caster derives from OE meaning "camp" or some type of "fortification". **"Mun.."** possibly comes from ON, referring to a "point" or a "headland". "The fortification at the point".

Muncaster Castle

Mungrisedale

A lovely sounding name. "**...grise..**" comes from ON for pigs, and "**...dale**" derives from ON for valley. There is debate about the first syllable. Possibly from a personal name, referring to St Mungo, an early saint, after whom numerous churches in the area are named. Maybe "Mungo's valley where the pigs feed".

TOWNS, VILLAGES AND AREAS.

Maiden Castle

One of several "Maiden Castles" in UK. Probably an Iron Age hill fort. The meaning of the fort's name is unclear, and it may have been previously called by another name. The use of "maiden" is also common throughout Europe.

Mains Farm
Mains is used to denote the main or home farm of an estate.

Meathop
Believed to be from OE, meaning the "middle portion of land".

Mediobodgum
The old name for the Roman Fort now called Hardknott. Probably from B, apparently meaning the "middle of the bend", though it is less than clear to what this refers.

Milkingstead
From OE, the "dairy farm".

Mill..
The word **"mill"** or "Miller" occurs very frequently. Almost all describe the "mill", the "miller" or occasionally someone called "Miller".

Milldam
From OE, describing the millpond, from which water ran to drive the mill-wheel.

Moota
Outside the national park, but with the same derivation as Muthill in Perthshire. Derived from OE , meaning the "meeting hill".

Normoss
A combination of OE and ON, the "northernmost marsh"

MOUNTAINS, FELLS AND VALLEYS
Nan Bield Pass
Joan Lee suggests this name means the "pass of the shelter". Whaley argues for a pass named after a shelter owned by someone called Anne.

TOWNS, VILLAGES AND AREAS
Newbiggin
"New…" is self-evident. **"…biggin"** derives from ON meaning "building" or "farmstead". The "new farmstead".

Newlands
Self-explanatory. Describes land which has been brought into use through clearing, or in the case of the valley bottom, through drainage.

Norfolk Island
The small island at the southern end of Ullswater, named after the Duke of Norfolk.

Norfolk Island

NAMES BEGINNING WITH "N"

RIVERS AND LAKES
Naddle Beck
"Na…" possibly from a number of sources. Most attractive is Diana Whaley's suggestion that it is ON, describing the "wedge shape" of the **"…ddle"**, derived from ON meaning "valley". **"Beck"** from ON meaning stream. The "stream in the wedge-shaped valley".

RIVERS AND LAKES
Overwater
"Over…" Unrelated to the modern usage of "over". More likely to derive from ON, referring to the "grouse", and **"..water"** meaning "lake". The "lake where you find grouse".

Local property named after the lake

MOUNTAINS, FELLS AND VALLEYS
Oak Head
The top of the oak wood.
Oak How
Almost self explanatory. Meaning the "hill", from ON, "where there are oak trees".
Old Man of Coniston
The most prominent summit in the southern lakes. It is suggested that this required a certain respect, which was given by the term **"Old"**. It is further suggested that the use of "Man" is merely a literary device. (For Coniston see letter C)
Owsen Fell
"Owsen" derives from a Cumbrian form of the usual word "oxen". **"Fell"** from ON meaning "hill". The "hill where the oxen have pasture".
Oxendale
The "valley ON where the oxen are pastured".

Over Cave
Above the cave or cove.

TOWNS, VILLAGES AND AREAS.
Old Scales
"Scales" is a common name, derived in most cases from ON, meaning "summer pasture" or "shieling". The "old summer pastures", which perhaps have now been abandoned.
Ore Gap
"Gap" refers to a mountain pass, and **"Ore"** probably derives from OE, referring to "ore", either found there or transported through the gap.
Ormathwaite
Changed from its early spelling of "Nordmanthait", when it clearly meant the "clearing of the Norseman" or "Norwegian".

More descriptive local names

Orthwaite
"Or…" possibly derives from ON, meaning "higher". **"…thwaite"** is from the ubiquitous ON meaning "clearing". The "higher clearing".
Ouse Bridge
"Bridge" is obviously ME, and **"Ouse"** is likely derived from an ancient Brit word, which describes "water".

RIVERS AND LAKES

Paddigill
"Paddi..." is likely to be derived by the Cumbrian dialect for "frog" or "toad". Although "...gill" suggests "stream", it is likely that the earliest name was influenced by the ON word for "spring". Probably the" spring where you find frogs or toads".

Priest Pot
Probably means "priest's pool", with a host of suggested derivations.

MOUNTAINS, FELLS AND VALLEYS

Penn, The
Brit/Cumbric for "hill".

Picket Howe
"The hill which comes to a pointed summit", as in "Pike" (below). Both from ON.

Pikeawassa
"Pike..." from ON, referring to the "pointed summit" and "...awassa", probably derived from a personal name, maybe "Wat". "Wat's sharp pointed summit".

Langdale Pikes - many hills are called "pikes"

Pike de Bield
"Pike" ON for summit. "de" from Fr, and "Bield" meaning a "lair" or "den", the place where an animal stayed. The "summit of the den".

Pike of Blisco
Obviously a "summit", but the meaning of Blisco remains a problem.

Pike of Stickle
One of the Lake District's most important archaeological sites, the location of the Neolithic axe "factory" which, it is believed supplied much of Britain and Ireland. "**Pike**" from ON refers to the sharp summit; "**Stickle**" is believed to derived from OE, describing the "steep mountain". The "pointed summit of the steep mountain".

Plumgarth
"**Plum..**" from OE, referring to the fruit. "**...garth**" is ON for some sort of "enclosure" or "orchard". Simply means the "plum orchard".

Pye Howe
A mixture of a ME word for "magpie" and ON for "hill". The "hill where you find magpies".

TOWNS, VILLAGES AND AREAS

Paddock Wray
"**Paddock**" or "**puddick**" was a dialect word still in use in Cumbria in the author's childhood, and is still used in Scotland, meaning "a frog or toad". "**Wray**", from ON, normally infers something which is "secluded" or "remote". The "remote place where you can find frogs or toads".

Park
"**Park**" is a common part of a name, and occurs with Beck, Gate, Nook and many other words. It usually refers to large areas which had been enclosed or set aside for hunting, though they

would also likely be used as normal pasture.

Parkend
The "end of the hunting enclosure".

Parkgate
The "gate to the hunting enclosure".

Peel Island
"Peel" probably relates to a "peel tower" ME. "A fortified tower house".

Peggy's Bridge
Who was Peggy? One of the newest names. Peggy was the wife of Denis Webb-Jones, who was responsible for the bridge over Warnscale Beck, built in 1991 a year after Peggy's death.

Penrith
An ancient name. "Pen..." is derived from a B word meaning "head" or "top". "...rith" is thought to be derived from a Cumbric word meaning "ford". But which ford? Across the River Eamont, or the Lowther, or even the Eden to the east? It seems that Penrith may have been located in a different place originally. Perhaps in the vicinity of Mayburgh Henge maybe.
The "headland by the ford".

Penruddock
A lovely name, but one with an uncertain meaning. The first part of the name may have a similar origin and meaning to Penrith, but it is uncertain what the meaning of the final element originally referred to.

Ullswater steamer near Pooley Bridge

Pooley Bridge
Probably derived from OE, describing the site of the bridge beside a "pool" in the River Eamont, as it flows out of Ullswater.

Portinscale
An unusual name. The first element "Portin.". is believed to come from ON , and it is suggested that it referred to "prostitutes". "...scale" obviously also comes from ON, the word for "shieling" or "the hut at the shieling". So the likely meaning is the "prostitutes' hut at the shieling".

Portinscale

Priorling
"Prior..." relates to Calder Abbey to the southwest. "...ling" is most likely from the ON word for "heather". One must assume the area was originally covered in heather.

THE ONLY "Q" WORD

Quagrigg Moss
Both the elements "Quag.." and also "Moss" refer to a bog, especially a "peat moss". "Rigg" is from ON for "ridge". The "boggy ridge".

RIVERS AND LAKES

Raise Beck

"Raise", ON for "cairn". **"Beck"** ON for "stream". The "stream beside the cairn".

Rothay River

There is some debate over the name of this river which flows into Windermere at Ambleside.

"...ay" is from ON, meaning a "river", and **"Roth..."** may derive from various possibilities, with the consensus being an association with trout. Possibly the "river with trout".

Bridge over River Rothay

Routenbeck

"Routen..." occurs in several names and may come from OE or ON, meaning "roaring", plus **"...beck"**, from ON, meaning a "stream". Possibly roaring streams are associated with waterfalls or for some reason they are noisy.

MOUNTAINS, FELLS AND VALLEYS

Raise

"Raise" derives from an ON word which means "cairn", usually a pile of stones, originally over a burial cist, a "box" made of stone slabs.

Rake Crags

The "rocky cliffs beside the path".

Ramp Holme

"Ramp" is from OE for "rams" or "male sheep". **"Holme"** from ON for "island". The "island where the rams pasture".

Randy Pike

"Randy" is likely a shortened form of Randolph, plus **"Pike"**, meaning a "pointed summit".

Raven Crag

"Raven" is very common in Lake District names, deriving from either OE or ON." **Crag"** refers to "rocky cliffs" or "outcrops" and from the frequency of Raven Crags or similar, it would suggest that ravens were very common.

Ravenglass

There are varying opinions on this name, best known as the western start of the famous narrow-gauge railway. Its first version appeared during the 13th century, so the name is very old. Possibly means "Glas's portion or share", though there are numerous other interpretations.

One of the icons of the Lake District

Red Howe

"Red" is a common element in names, and may mean the colour "red", or in some cases, refers to OE , meaning "reeds". We find Red Screes, Red Tarn,

Red Syke and numerous others. Red Howe is likely to be simply "red hill".

Rigg Beck
"Rigg" derives from ON for "ridge", and "Beck", also ON, meaning "stream". The "stream next to the ridge".

Riggindale
"Riggin.." is probably from ON meaning "ridge", and "...dale" refers to "valley". Probably the "valley below the ridge".

Rosset Crag/Gill
"Rosset" is thought to be derived from a combination of two ON words, which together refer to "summer pasture for horses". "Crag" describes a "rocky outcrop" and "Gill" a "stream".

Round Howe
Likely describing a "round-topped hill".

Rowantree Crag
Simply the "crag where you find rowan trees". There are other examples where the rowan tree is invoked in a name.

TOWNS, VILLAGES AND AREAS.
Raisethwaite
"Raise.." from OE meaning "cairn" and "...thwaite", meaning "clearing". The "clearing where you find a cairn".

Rake
"Rake" derives from ON and usually refers to a "track".

Riddings, The
"Ridding" from OE, means a "clearing", like the ON-derived element "thwaite". It occurs in numerous names.

Roger Ground
This and similar names refers to "land" or a "farm" belonging to someone with a personal name, in this case "Roger".

Rosthwaite
"Ross..." derived from ON, meaning "horses" and "thwaite" a "clearing". The "clearing with horses".

Ruthwaite
"Ruth..." is possibly from OE meaning "rough" and "....thwaite", ON for "clearing". The "rough clearing".

Rydal
"Ry..." from OE for the cereal "rye", and "...dal", from ON for "valley". The "valley where rye grows".

Rydal Water

Places are often named after people

46

LAKES AND RIVERS

Simon Kell

"**Kell**" ON describes a "spring". "**Simon**" is originally from the personal name "**Sigmund**". "The spring of Sigmund".

Skelghyll

Whaley suggests there are two alternative ways, both ON, to describe this "**...ghyll**" near Ambleside. One is that it refers to a location beside a "summer pasture" or "shieling". Otherwise it may describe a "roaring stream", as one might find in a rocky ghyll or ravine.

"Stream beside the shieling"

Skelwith (or ..bridge, ..fold, ..force etc)

"**Skel...**" derives from ON, meaning "noisy" and "**...with**" derives from a word meaning a "ford" across a river. Commentators suggest that the "noise" refers to the adjacent waterfall of Skelwith Force.

Smithy Beck

Self-explanatory. Alongside this beck, or stream, iron ore was refined.

Sour Milk Gill

This descriptive name probably requires very little explanation. There are many examples of this favoured description for a foaming, white cascade, rushing down the mountain.

Spout Force

"**Spout**", a similar Gaelic name appears frequently in Scotland in the form of "sput" (eg "Sput Rolla" near Comrie). "**Force**" comes from ON for "waterfall". Suggests a "cascading waterfall". Perhaps another example of "Waterfall waterfall".

Sprinkling Tarn

"**Tarn**" ON meaning "mountain pond" or "small lake". "**Sprinkling**" probably from OE meaning "sparkling".

Stickle Tarn

"**Tarn**" from ON meaning "mountain pond" and "**Stickle**" means a pointed hill or mountain. The "mountain pond below the pointed mountain".

MOUNTAINS, FELLS AND VALLEYS

Saddleback

The name "**Saddleback**" appears to have been used since the 18th century, and describes the "saddle-shape" between the peaks of the "chair-shaped" summit of Blencathra.

Saddleback

St John's in the Vale

Named after the church of St John the Baptist, dating from the 13th century.

St John's in the Vale

St Raven's Edge

One of those interesting words which have mutated over time. Unlikely to be related either to a "saint" or to "ravens". Probably derived from the ON word for "shieling" or "summer pasture", but changed over the years. Plus "**Edge**", meaning an escarpment.

St Sunday Crag

Named after St Dominic, who was also called St Sunday.

Sca Fell Pike

England's highest mountain. "**Sca**" may derive from ON meaning "bald" or "bare", though some suggest that it could also refer to "shielings" or "summer pastures". "**Fell**" and "**Pike**" describe the mountain and the summit.

Scandale

"**Scan...**" is likely from ON, meaning "short", with "**...dale**" meaning "valley". The "short valley".

Scar

Generally refers to an exposed escarpment, usually limestone. There are many examples, "**Scar..**" with Crag, Foot, ...green, head etc.

Scarth Gap

"**Scarth**" is probably deived from ON, meaning a "col", the pass between two hills or parts of a hill. So "Scarth Gap Pass" effectively means "gap, gap, gap".

Seat

The name "**Seat**" is common, and has two possible derivations, both ON. Most common is probably "summer pasture" or "shieling". Alternatively it can mean "seat" as in Modern English, or simply a "high place".

Sharp Edge

An aptly, and fairly recently named glacially-formed arête on Blencathra, also called Razor Edge.

Shundraw

By no means clear as to its meaning, but Whaley suggests "lookout hill" as her best guess.

Silver Crag

Whether the various Lake District names including "silver" actually refer to the metal is unclear. Some appear to be personal names; others refer to legends and others to plants. Why the name "Silver Crag" is unclear.

Skiddaw

One of Lakeland's peaks over 3000 feet. The suggested meaning, from ON, of the mountain with the "jutting crag" seems unlikely. The author looked on Skiddaw daily during his childhood, and saw smooth slopes devoid of the jutting crags of Borrowdale. It would seem that the meaning is obscure.

Skiddaw shrouded in cloud

Slate Hill
In spite of the importance of slate in the Lake District, this is the only name which includes it. Self-explanatory.

Stang
ON referring to a "ridge".

Steel End
"Steel" comes from ON for "steep". Probably the "end of the steep ridge".

Steeple
Possibly a name from OE, but likely more recent. Refers to the "spire-like shape " of this particular rock.

Sticks Pass
Possibly from OE, describing a "pass marked with sticks".

Striding Edge
One of the Lake District's most famous locations, part of the horse-shoe corrie and arêtes at the summit of Helvellyn. **"Edge"** refers to the sharp arête; **"Striding"** derives from ON and the meaning here is not very clear, unless it refers to Striding Edge as a "path", ie where you can take "strides".

Stybarrow Crag
"Sty" from ON meaning "a steep track". **"...barrow"** meaning "hill". **"Crag"** refers to a rocky cliff.

Sty Head
Meaning, the "head of the pass", from Borrowdale into Wasdale.

TOWNS, VILLAGES AND PLACES
Saltcoats
"Salt..." from ON word for "salt", plus **"...coats"**, an OE word for "cottage". Probably meaning "the place where salt was stored, after being made by evaporation along the coast.

Sampson's Bratfull
Interesting sounding name. There are legends about Samson from the Bible carrying stones in an apron, which subsequently broke and spilled the stones. Possibly Sampson, plus B word for "apron".

Sandwick
From ON words meaning "sand" and "bay". "Sandy bay".

The village of Satterthwaite

Satterthwaite
A lovely ON combination which seems to typify the settlement of the Scandinavians as they moved into the interior of Lakeland. **"Satter."**. probably from the word for "shieling" or "summer pasture" and **"...thwaite"** meaning clearing". "The clearing at the summer pasture". It is now a village.

Sawrey Ground
Simply the land of the Sawrey family.

The land belonging to the Sawrey family

49

Seathwaite

Seathwaite, in Borrowdale is reputed to be England's wettest place. 13th and 14th century records suggest that the name derives from ON meaning "sedge" and the ubiquitous "..**thwaite**", referring to "clearing. "The clearing where sedge grows".

Seatoller

There is some disagreement amongst scholars about this name. Located at the foot of Honister Pass, it most likely refers to a "shieling" or "summer pasture". However, whether the last element refers to "elders" or to a personal name is unknown.

Swinside Stone Circle

Seaton

From ON, meaning "steading or hamlet near or by the sea".

Shap

The location of both the famous granite, much loved by Neolithic monument builders, and also of the village situated at the high point of one of UK's most important routeways. Probably from OE, meaning "the pile of stones". Though the first recorded written mention is in the 13th century, the Shap area was the location for many Neolithic and bronze age circles and stone rows. So possibly the "pile of stones" is much older than OE.

Sillathwaite

Probably derived from an ON personal name, plus "...**thwaite**".

Sleddale

From a combination of OE and ON, both elements of this name mean "valley". Technically it is believed the meaning is the "valley with the tributary valley".

Snittlegarth

Quaint sounding name. Possibly the "enclosure" or "field" associated with "snaring", probably of rabbits.

Southwaite

There are differences over the meaning of this name. "...**thwaite**" is from ON, meaning a "clearing", but there are different suggestions among scholars as to whether the first element, "**South...**" refers to "south" (as in Modern E), something related to "sheep" , or to a "muddy pool", the latter two from ON.

Stanegarth

ON for "stony field" or "enclosure".

Staveley

From OE referring to "staffs" or "poles". Probably the "clearing or place where staffs or poles were obtained".

Stoneraise

"**Stone**" "stony" or "rocky". "...**raise**", "cairn" or "burial mound".

Stonethwaite

The "stony clearing"

Swinside

"**Swin**" from OE or ON (the same word) means "pigs", with "...**side**" probably from ON, meaning "summer pasture". There are also other possibilities, referring to "hillside with pigs" and "high places with pigs ".

Syke Beck

"**Syke**" ON, usually a "slow-moving stream". "**Beck**" refers to a "stream".

RIVERS AND LAKES

Tarn

"Tarn" ON, refers to a "small lake" or "large pond" usually in the mountains, though not always. Many tarns are almost as famous as the major lakes.

Tarn Hows

Though this name is actually used for the small lake between Hawkshead and Coniston, literally it refers to the nearby hills. "Tarn" from ON for a "pond" and "Hows" from ON refer to "hills". The "hills beside the small lake".

Tewet Tarn

"Tewet" derives from early dialect for "lapwing", together with "Tarn", from ON, for "small mountain lake". The "small lake where you get lapwings".

Thirlmere

Different commentators come up with varying explanations, ranging from "lake in a hollow" to "narrow-waisted lake", to a possible connection with a personal name. Until the 18th century, Thirlmere was actually called "Leathes-water". The lake in its present form dates only from 1840.

Thirlmere

Thorngill Beck

"Thorn..." usually from ON and it is believed to refer to "hawthorn". "...gill" describes a "ravine" or "gorge" as the stream (Beck) rushes down from the fells. The " stream in the ravine with hawthorn trees".

Trout Beck

The "stream which has trout".

MOUNTAINS, FELLS AND VALLEYS

Tod Fell

"Tod" is derived from ON/OE, meaning "fox". Tod Fell was the "hill where you find foxes", though foxes are found all over the Lake District, even today.

Trusmadoor

The pass or col between Great Cockup and Meal Fell. "Trusma..." derives from a C word meaning a "door" or "pass". It seems likely that "...door" was added later, with the meaning repeated.

TOWNS, VILLAGES AND AREAS

Thackthwaite

"Thack..." ON, means "thatch" and "...thwaite" is a "clearing". The "clearing where you find thatching material".

Threlkeld

"Threl..." from ON means a "serf" or "slave", with "...keld", describing a "spring". The "spring of the serf".

Threlkeld

Throstle Garth
"Throstle" is still used in local dialect today for "thrush", and derives from OE. "**Garth**" ON, means an "enclosure". The "enclosure of the thrush".

Thwaite
The commonest single name or name element found in the Lake District. From ON, meaning "clearing", gives evidence of the part played by settlers from Iceland and western Norway 1000 years ago.

Torver
Likely ON, a personal name meaning "Torfi's shieling " or "summer pasture". However, "torfi" may refer to "peat cutting" or "turfs", so simply refers to the material from which it was made.

The way to "Torfi's shieling" perhaps

Tottle Bank
From OE meaning the "hill from which you peeped out", or in more common English, the "lookout hill".

Tranthwaite
"Tran..." is from ON, meaning a "crane" or a "heron", and "**...thwaite**", a "clearing". The "clearing where you find cranes or herons".

Troutal
Combination of OE and ON, meaning the "trout pond".

Tullythwaite
Probably the "Tillaug's clearing".

NAMES BEGINNING WITH "U"

The elements "**Ul...**"or "**Ull...**" occur commonly and are generally attributed to ON for "wolf". There is debate as to the date of the "last wolf in Britain" but certainly there were wolves here until about the end of the 17th century, maybe a little later.

LAKES AND RIVERS

Ullswater
"**Ulls..**" is possibly related to a personal name, though also maybe to ON for "wolf". The "lake of the wolves" or perhaps "Ulf's lake".

The steamer on Ullswater

Undermillbeck
The suggestion is that in this case "**Under...**" means "south of". "**...mill...**" derives from OE for "mill" and "**...beck**" from ON meaning "stream". The "stream south of the mill".

MOUNTAINS, FELLS AND VALLEYS

Ullscarf
Unclear. Possibly from ON meaning "the pass of the wolves"

Underbarrow
"**...barrow**" from OE meaning "hill", and "**under**" for the "place below the hill".

TOWNS, VILLAGES AND AREAS
Uldale
North Lakes village. Debate over when "Ul…" is a personal name, or refers to ON "wolves". "**Dale…**" from ON, meaning "valley". The "valley of the wolves" is the nicer choice.

Ulpha
Parish named after the hill. From ON, meaning "wolf hill".

Uzzicar
There is some discussion over this name. From ON or OE, and relating to cultivated land beside a building.

NAMES BEGINNING WITH "V"

A few names begin with "v"

LAKES AND RIVERS
Victoria Bay
Named after Queen Victoria.

MOUNTAINS, FELLS AND VALLEYS
Vaugh Steel
"**Steel**" probably from ON meaning a "steep place", but there is little understanding of "**Vaugh**". Maybe "clearing".

NAMES BEGINNING WITH "W"

LAKES AND STREAMS
Wastwater
A repetition of names, combing ON and modern English, literally meaning the "The lake of the valley with a lake (or water)".

Water Yeat
The "sluice gate", as in a corn mill water course. From OE.

White Gill
The "gorge with the milk-like stream".

Whit Beck
Probably from a combination of OE and ON meaning the "stream where you find willows".

Whitewater Dash
The spectacular white cascade on the northern side of Skiddaw.

Windermere
The biggest lake in England. Probably after a personal name "**Vinandr**", and "**…mere**", one of the common names for "lake". "Vinand's Lake".

Windermere in the early morning

MOUNTAINS, FELLS AND VALLEYS
Wadcrag
"**Wad…**" several meanings, but most likely is Cumbrian dialect for "graphite".

Waingap
"Wain..." from OE, meaning a "wagon", together with **"..gap"**, referring to a "pass". The "pass used by wagons".

Walna Scar
"Scar" from ON , usually referring to a carboniferous outcrop. Joan Lee suggests that the name is totally from ON, meaning the "hill of the British".

Wasdale
"Was..." may refer to an ON personal name, or may refer to an ON word meaning "water" or "lake"."**...dale"**, from ON, meaning "valley". Probably the "valley with a lake".

Watch Hill
Most likely a "lookout hill" from which it was possible to get an early view of raiders from Scotland.

Watson's Dodd
The hill named after a certain Watson.

Whelp Side
From ON. Possibly the side of the hill associated with young wolves.

Whin
ON for "gorse", an element found in many names. Still used as the normal dialect in Cumbria and many parts of Scotland.

Whin Fell
ON, The "hill where you find gorse".

Whinlatter
The pass and forest between Braithwaite and Lorton. A combination of the ON for "gorse" and" **...latter"**, derived from a G word meaning a "pass". The "pass where the gorse grows".

Willie Wife Moor
A references to wives dating from at least the 17th century. Origin unknown.

Windy Gap
The col between Great Gable and Green Gable. Diana Whaley suggests

A popular visit for families

that the name originally didn't have its present connotation, but its modern meaning is very apt.

Withe Bottom
From OE, the "valley with willow trees".

Wrynose Pass
Probably derived from ON meaning "stallion", or at least a powerful horse and **"pass"**, suggesting that only strong horses could manage it.

TOWNS, VILLAGES AND AREAS
Wabberthwaite
"Wabber..." ON probably a "fishing or hunting shed or hut" where you might briefly stay when you are fishing or hunting. **"...thwaite"**, meaning "clearing". So, the "clearing with a fishing or hunting hut or shed".

Wallthwaite
"Wall..." is most likely derived from OE and refers to the "fulling" of cloth. **"...thwaite"** is ON for a "clearing". The "clearing where fulling takes place". ("Fulling" is cleansing, shrinking and thickening cloth by application of moisture, heat and pressure). Joan Lee suggests more simply, from ON the "clearing beside the wall".

Wanthwaite
"Wan..." is most likely derived from an ON word for angelica". The "clearing where you find angelica".

Watendlath

Complicated name with elements from several language influences including ON and OE. Thought to describe a barn at the end of Watendlath Tarn. The "barn at the end of the lake".

Watendlath Tarn

Watermillock

Earliest records do not show "**Water...**", but an ON element meaning "sheep". It is likely that "**...millock**" is from a diminutive form in Cumbric, meaning "little hill", "little bald" or "bare hill". The "little bare hill where sheep graze".

Westmorland

Originally referred to the "moorland to the west", presumably "west of the Pennines". Westmorland was a separate county until local government reorganisation in 1974.

Whinscales

From ON, the "summer pasture where the gorse grows".

Wray Castle

"**Wray**" derived from ON, referring to a "remote place", presumably on the other side of the lake. Wray Castle is recent, a folly, built in the 19th century.

Wythop

Most likely from OE meaning the "valley with willows".

NAMES BEGINNING WITH "Y"

LAKES AND RIVERS

Yew Tree Tarn

The "pool with yew trees".

MOUNTAINS, FELLS AND VALLEYS

Yarlside

"**Yarl...**" derives from ON meaning "chieftain" or "lord" (the meaning as in Scottish laird), and "**...side**" from ON meaning "seat" or "vantage point".

Yewbarrow

Early records suggest that the "**Yew...**" in this name refers to "sheep" rather than the tree. "**...barrow**" is a "hill". The "hill where ewes graze".

Yew tree berries

Yewdale

In comparison with Yewbarrow (above), the oldest records confirm this name as referring to "yew trees" rather than sheep. The "valley where there are yew trees".

Yew Pike

The "mountain with yew trees".

If you wish to take your interest further

There are only a few other books on the subject, but fortunately the English Place Names Society published a superb, but expensive dictionary on Lake District names in 2006, written by Diana Whaley, Professor of Early Medieval Studies at Newcastle University. As you might expect, it is a most learned study, pursuing Lake District names to their earliest recorded mention, identifying linguistic origins and subsequent changes. Available at most good bookshops at about £20.

A Dictionary of Lake District Place Names: Diana Whaley

Other sources worth pursuing include:-

The Place Names of Cumbria: Joan Lee

Lake District Place Names: Robert Gambles

Web-site of the Institute of Place Names
www.nottingham.ac.uk/english/research/ch/CENS/about/html

There are also numerous interesting websites
which you might "Google" using "Cumbrian"
or "Lake District place names"